Testament

poems

Testament

poems

Luke Hankins

TRP: The University Press of SHSU
Huntsville, Texas

Library of Congress Cataloging-in-Publication Data

Names: Hankins, Luke, 1984- author.
Title: Testament : poems / Luke Hankins.
Description: First edition. | Huntsville : TRP: The University Press of
  SHSU, [2023]
Identifiers: LCCN 2022039062 (print) | LCCN 2022039063 (ebook) |
ISBN
  9781680033304 (paperback) | ISBN 9781680033311 (ebook)
Subjects: LCSH: Psychic trauma--Poetry. | Revelation--Poetry. | LCGFT:
  Poetry.
Classification: LCC PS3608.A715 T47 2023 (print) | LCC PS3608.A715
  (ebook) | DDC 811/.6--dc23/eng/20220822
LC record available at https://lccn.loc.gov/2022039062
LC ebook record available at https://lccn.loc.gov/2022039063

Cover design and interior design by Miranda Ramírez

Cover Image: *The Prodigal Son*, Honoré Daumier,
courtesy of The National Gallery of Art

Printed and bound in the United States of America

Published by TRP: The University Press of SHSU
Huntsville, Texas 77341
texasreviewpress.org

Table of Contents

Category Error

Hummingbirds are fighting
over the flowers in the garden again,
because beauty doesn't make anything
immune to cruelty.

Imagine a world in which each
beautiful creature could be trusted—
and isn't each creature beautiful?

The sleek, streaked coat of the tiger.
The iridescent scales of the snake.
The shockingly blue eyes
of the shooter on the evening news.

No Sculpted Stone

Storm-havoc in the pines
        makes fragrant air.

            Incense of breakage,
    music of demise.

      Here is my cathedral,

wounded, trying
       to heal—
           its splinters

     mirror splinters
         in me.

Hum

Though we were poor at touch
as a family, my father would blow on my face
to cool me in the heat of Louisiana summers,
upstairs in church where he ran the sound board.

It was the sweetest shock—
as if the Holy Ghost had swept
straight through me, leaving
my spine full of static.

His breath hums in me still.

The Answer

On some sacred page all the answers lie curled
like embryos waiting to be born.
In the meantime I'm trying to understand the world.

Every second hungry bullets are hurled,
seeking whom they may devour. Be warned.
(Where's that sacred page where all the answers lie curled?)

Out of love Confederate flags are unfurled
on trucks roaring through our towns.
Or maybe I've misunderstood the world.

We've armed everyone and are assured
threats are neutralized on a balanced battleground.
(In which ammo case do the instructions lie curled?)

The handle of my gun is beautiful—filigreed and pearled.
(The business end doesn't need to be adorned
to be adored.) The answer to your question? It's curled
around the sacred bullet flying through the world.

Procession

An ambulance appears over a hill, lights and sirens blaring. It's moving slowly. Cars make way as it maneuvers through the town. Confused drivers peer through the ambulance window at the uniformed man behind the wheel who is concentrating on the road he's traveling slow yard by slow yard. He looks as if he might be sweating. The wailing doesn't modulate in pitch as everyone has come to expect from an ambulance racing to someone's aid. It remains for unbearably long minutes, the keening of an inconsolable mother for a child, the rabid howl of the demon-possessed. A trail of frozen traffic lingers in the wake. The driver sweats, gripping the wheel, staring straight ahead. Where will it stop? When will it end? On and on, the terrible chariot blazes its path.

Wave Function

I walked outside
into two days at once.
East, dense cloud-cover.
West, blazing sun.

As if I could choose
which day I would
participate in.

I couldn't move,
right eye squinting
against hot radiance,
left ear catching thunder.

Limit

No longer will I see Roman cathedrals,
Tibetan monasteries, Caribbean reefs,
the Grand Canyon.

I live in a small town
and can't get out,
though not for the usual reasons.

Traveling makes me
panic—marrow-deep.
I'm cut off

from the usual glories.
But sometimes I drive the bridge
over our river—not a broad river,

not a huge bridge—and see the town
spread out, somewhat below me.
It is a very small glory.

Nevertheless

You think you're saying the right thing.
And then they step into the bathroom
and induce vomiting.

The marks on their forehead and neck,
self-inflicted,
refuse your care.

The world spins
madly on, and I'm mad
at the world.

I have seen the rarest of lives
wish with every cell it was composed of
that it was over.

I have lain soundless in awesome sorrow
next to a heart that wanted nothing more
than to stop.

And there were
no adequate
words.

And I spoke.

Synapse

To hypothesize

is the luxury

of philosophers and poets—

a privilege the man in Beirut

who tackled the suicide bomber

last week did not share

when he made

the decision

to die

for those around him.

To be
or not
to be—

synaptically

the quandary

lasts milliseconds—

in it is no philosophy,

only an instinct

greater than any poetry.

Say I Am Not Damned

I am not good enough for God.

I could not give up
the balm for my anxiety—

                                 bane in other ways.

The God of strict account
has weighed my thoughts and deeds.
And there was never any chance.

I think both too much of myself
and too little.

                    Ditto God.

                    And all of you.

There's an answer that keeps calling my name
because it's lost,

                    or I am.

God asked me if I wanted to be a saint.
I said hell no.

                  No one can identify with a saint—
not even You.

My ego has grown large
because its protective shell cracked apart.

Sometimes I think I'm a god.
                                 And then I have to piss.

Am I not
a better servant
tipsy?

        I tip my hat to Thee.

        I sigh my songs to Thee.

        I love the broken world better
        that has broken me.

Visit

Enter, doubt. Come, remorse.
I detect your shadows beneath the door.
I can no longer bear
to leave you hovering there,
just outside, perhaps prepared
to resort to force.
I throw the lock, and I am scared.

Perspective

The purpose of every last
object, creature, molecule, entity
in our immeasurable universe
is to transform its own energy
into another kind, ad infinitum
and in saecula saeculorum, amen.

A universe utterly averse to stasis.

And where does your desire for immortality fit
in a cosmos predicated on loss?
(Gain, too—but not for you.)
Better to commit yourself to decay,
try to find beauty in it. And if *you* can't,
it may at least seem beautiful to another, far away.

Testament

I haven't lived terribly well—
but I probably haven't lived terribly, either.

I have often helplessly loved living.

I could say that much,
called to some celestial account.

I have, though dragged
like a defeated corpse

behind the night-gilded chariot
of despair for a time

that seemed timeless,

just as surely fallen at the hands
of beauty, plain delight—utter

surrender.

What We Have Made

What we have made is not melody,
but the memory of melody—
an elegy of imitation and frustrated desire,
he said. Shut up and sing it, she said.

My Name

Darkness, my name is Denis Johnson
–Denis Johnson, "Now"

Darkness, my name is Luke
—and that means light—

so it can't be near.
You've banished it.

Darkness, what is your name?
You so envelop it

within the folds of your being
that I'll never reach it.

You swallow me.
But not deeply enough.

My name is a pillar of fire
I remember but cannot see.

Darkness, swallow me,
swallow me.

I hear you are a gateway.

Prove it.

Acknowledgments

Anglican Theological Review:
  "No Sculpted Stone"
  "Testament"

Broad River Review:
  "Synapse"
  (Honorable Mention, 2019 Rash Award in Poetry)

Cutthroat:
  "What We Have Made"

EcoTheo Review:
  "Hum"

Misrepresented People: Poetic Responses to Trump's America
  (New York Quarterly Books, 2018):
  "The Answer"

The Montreal Prize Anthology 2020 (Canada: Signal Editions):
  "Category Error"
  (shortlisted for The 2020 Montreal International Poetry
  Prize)

About the Author

Luke Hankins is the author of two poetry collections, *Radiant Obstacles* and *Weak Devotions*, as well as a collection of essays, *The Work of Creation*. A volume of his translations from the French of Stella Vinitchi Radulescu, *A Cry in the Snow & Other Poems*, was released by Seagull Books in 2019. Hankins is the founder and editor of Orison Books, a non-profit literary press focused on the life of the spirit from a broad and inclusive range of perspectives.